The TARDIS doesn't look very hi-tech, but it can travel through time and space.

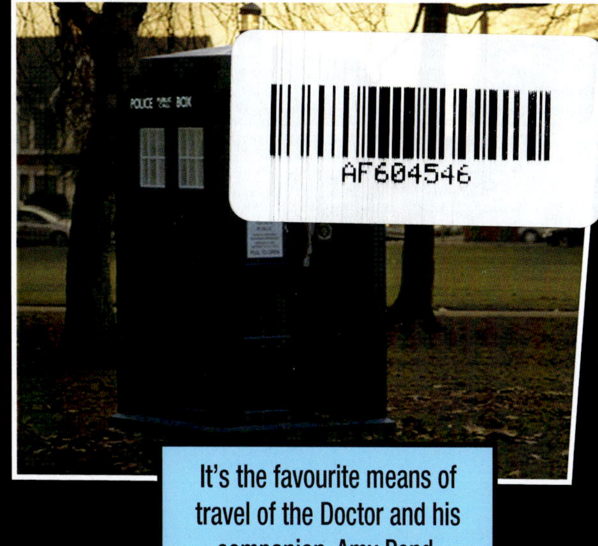

It's the favourite means of travel of the Doctor and his companion, Amy Pond.

The Lodger

Written by Peter Gutiérrez
Based on the television script "The Lodger"
by Gareth Roberts

Unknown to Amy, the Doctor has been thrown clear.

"– ARE YOU?"

Chapter 1: Stranded!

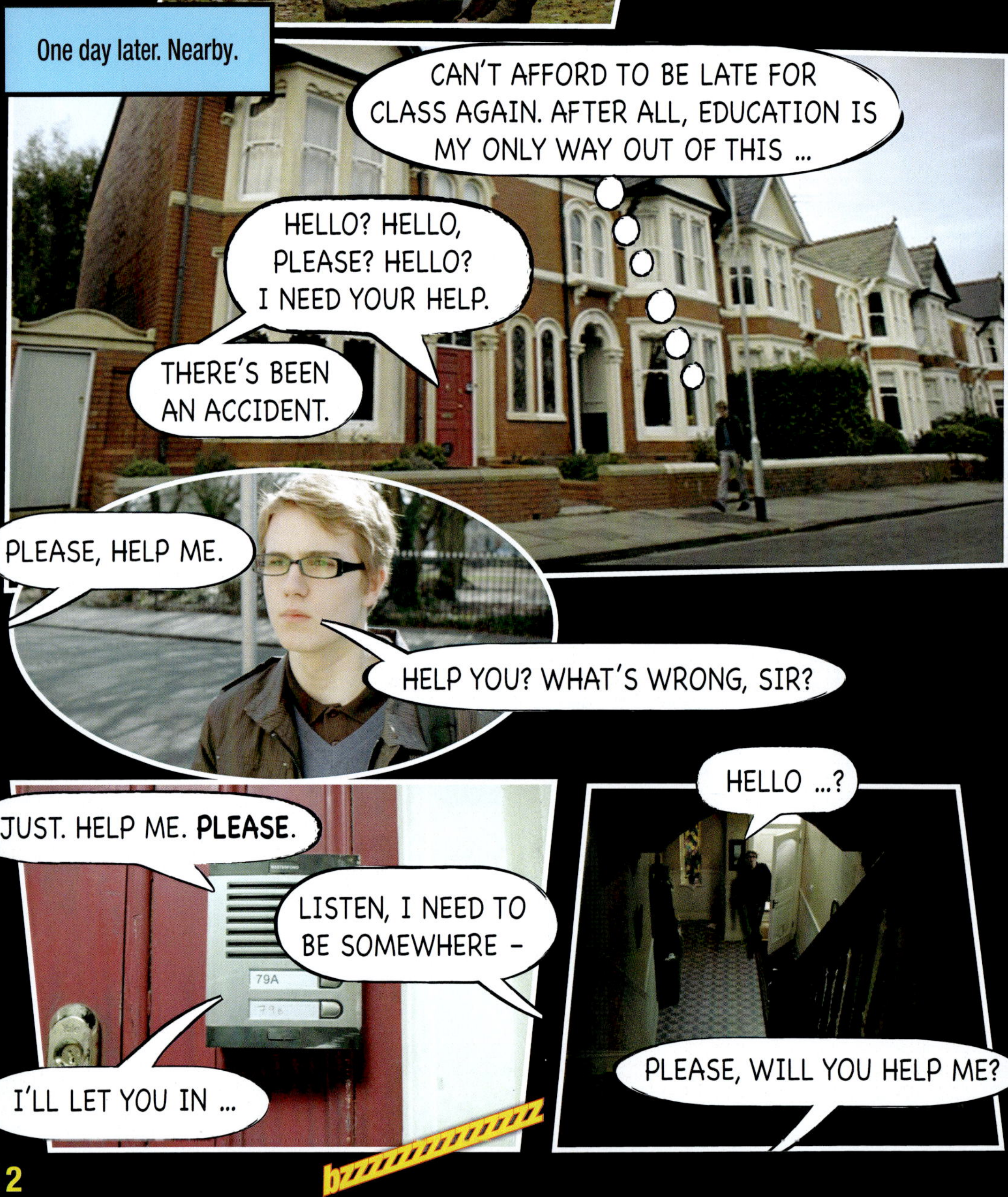

One day later. Nearby.

CAN'T AFFORD TO BE LATE FOR CLASS AGAIN. AFTER ALL, EDUCATION IS MY ONLY WAY OUT OF THIS ...

HELLO? HELLO, PLEASE? HELLO? I NEED YOUR HELP.

THERE'S BEEN AN ACCIDENT.

PLEASE, HELP ME.

HELP YOU? WHAT'S WRONG, SIR?

SOMETHING TERRIBLE HAS HAPPENED. PLEASE HELP ME.

With the lights flickering around him, the student climbs the stairs to help the older gentleman, who reminds him of his own grandfather.

In fact, he is so quick to help that he doesn't even notice that the door seems to close by itself behind him.

It's as if the student had never left a trace of his coming … or going. But he does leave a trace for those on the lower floor. It's a trace visible even to a casual visitor such as Sophie.
CRAIG, WHAT'S THAT ON THE CEILING?

WHAT'S WHAT ON THE CEILING?
THAT! IT'S COMING FROM UPSTAIRS. WHO LIVES UP THERE AGAIN?
JUST SOME GUY.
Craig is paying so much attention to the tea he's making – and to Sophie generally – that he doesn't even notice when the mysterious stain …
… spreads.

There is the faint sound of electricity buzzing somewhere in the house.

Their chat is interrupted by a call on Sophie's mobile phone.

NO, THAT'S ALL RIGHT. I SUPPOSE IT'S NOTHING REALLY IMPORTANT. IT'S JUST CRAIG.
Click
OH, THANKS, SOPH!

SORRY, CRAIG. THAT'S MELINA. SOUNDS LIKE ANOTHER CRISIS AND, YOU KNOW, WE HAD SETTLED ON JUST –
– JUST PIZZA AND TV, I KNOW. NO, YOU'RE RIGHT TO SPEND SOME TIME WITH HER.

REALLY? I COULD STAY.
SURE, IT'S FINE. I UNDERSTAND. SOME OTHER TIME.
WELL, THANKS. I REALLY APPRECIATE YOUR ... UNDERSTANDING.

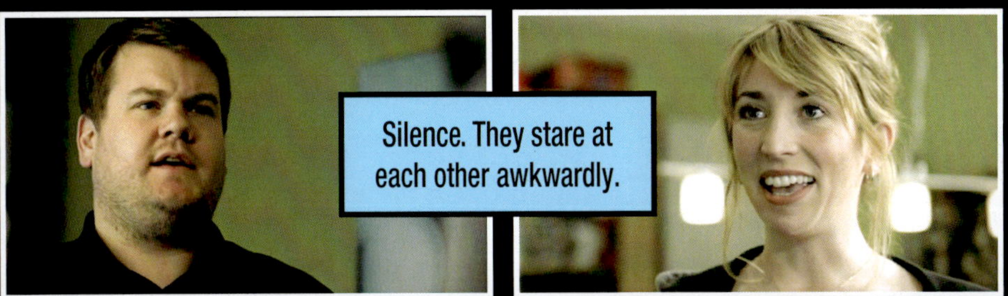
Silence. They stare at each other awkwardly.

On her way out, Sophie can't resist stealing a glance towards the upstairs flat.
WAIT, WHAT'S THAT? MOVEMENT? AS IF HE'S STANDING THERE WATCHING ALL DAY ... WAITING.

A few minutes later, Craig answers the front door.
brrrrriiiiiiiiiiiiiiiiiinnng!
MUST BE SOPHIE – LEFT HER KEYS BEHIND.
I AM AN IDIOT. WHY DON'T I JUST COME OUT AND TELL HER? WHAT'S SO HARD ABOUT SAYING ...

I LOVE YOU!
BUT I ONLY JUST PUT THE AD UP TODAY. AND I DIDN'T INCLUDE MY ADDRESS.

!!
WELL, THAT'S GOOD, SINCE I'M YOUR NEW LODGER. AND THANK YOU FOR THOSE KEYS. THIS IS GOING TO BE EASY!
WELL, AREN'T YOU LUCKY I CAME ALONG? LUCKIER THAN YOU KNOW.
HANG ON, MATE, I DON'T KNOW IF I WANT YOU STAYING. AND GIVE ME BACK THOSE KEYS.

YES, QUITE RIGHT. HAVE SOME RENT.
OH ...YES. IN THAT CASE ...
THAT'S PROBABLY QUITE A LOT. LOOKS LIKE A LOT. IS IT A LOT? I CAN NEVER TELL.

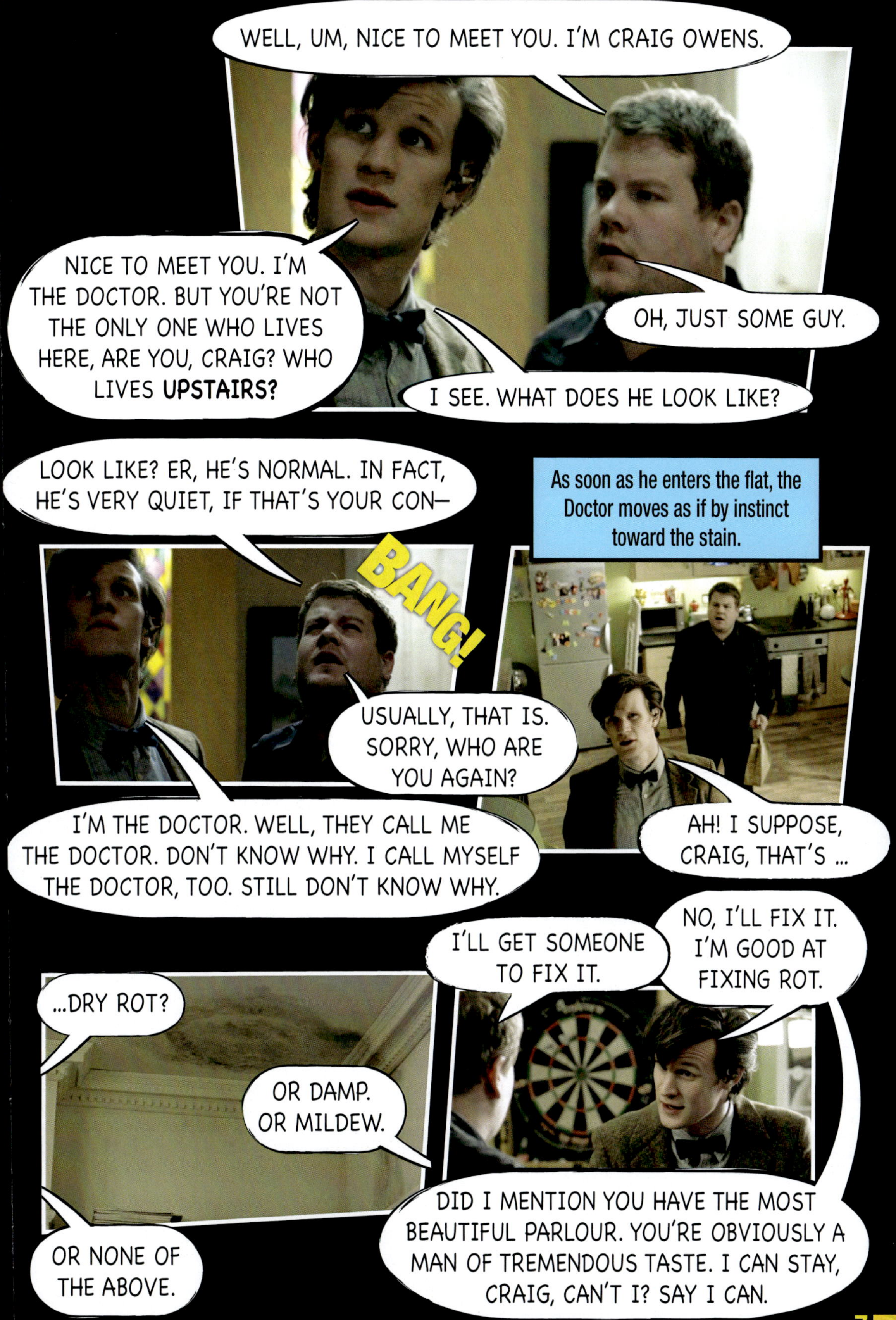

WELL, UM, NICE TO MEET YOU. I'M CRAIG OWENS.

NICE TO MEET YOU. I'M THE DOCTOR. BUT YOU'RE NOT THE ONLY ONE WHO LIVES HERE, ARE YOU, CRAIG? WHO LIVES **UPSTAIRS?**

OH, JUST SOME GUY.

I SEE. WHAT DOES HE LOOK LIKE?

LOOK LIKE? ER, HE'S NORMAL. IN FACT, HE'S VERY QUIET, IF THAT'S YOUR CON—

As soon as he enters the flat, the Doctor moves as if by instinct toward the stain.

AH! I SUPPOSE, CRAIG, THAT'S ...

I'LL GET SOMEONE TO FIX IT.

NO, I'LL FIX IT. I'M GOOD AT FIXING ROT.

DID I MENTION YOU HAVE THE MOST BEAUTIFUL PARLOUR. YOU'RE OBVIOUSLY A MAN OF TREMENDOUS TASTE. I CAN STAY, CRAIG, CAN'T I? SAY I CAN.

WHILE YOU'RE SAYING YES, I'LL MAKE US AN OMELETTE. BY THE WAY, WHO'S THE GIRL ON THE FRIDGE?
MY FRIEND. SOPHIE.
GIRLFRIEND?
ROCKS

A FRIEND WHO IS A GIRL. THERE'S NOTHING GOING ON.
AH, THAT WORKS FOR ME, TOO.
WE MET AT WORK ABOUT A YEAR AGO AT THE CALL CENTRE.

Meanwhile, Amy's frustration with the TARDIS grows …
OH, WHICH ONE, WHICH CONTROL?!

NO, NO, NO! WHY WON'T YOU LAND?!

… while the Doctor and Craig relax after enjoying an omelette.
OH, THAT WAS INCREDIBLE! WHERE DID YOU LEARN TO COOK?
PARIS, IN THE 18TH CENTURY.

Craig does his best to change the subject in a way that he hopes isn't obvious.

... ROT.

BY THE WAY, ABOUT THAT ROT ... I'VE GOT THE STRANGEST FEELING WE ...

SHOULDN'T TOUCH IT.

Chapter 2: "Are You Scared?"

SEE FOR YOURSELF. I MEAN, LISTEN FOR YOURSELF.

OOH, NASTY. SHE'S LOCKED IN A MATERIALISATION LOOP, TRYING TO LAND AGAIN.
THAT'S BAD. THAT COULD MEAN TIME ITSELF MIGHT START TO REPEAT.

NO SIGN OF THAT. MY READINGS SAY THAT WHATEVER'S STOPPING THE TARDIS IS UPSTAIRS IN THAT FLAT ...
... SO GO UPSTAIRS AND SORT IT!
I DON'T KNOW WHAT IT IS, THOUGH. ANYTHING THAT CAN STOP THE TARDIS FROM LANDING IS BIG.
SCARY BIG!

WAIT ... ARE YOU SCARED?
ME? OF COURSE NOT. BESIDES, I'VE GOT CRAIG HERE TO HELP ME.

... I MEAN, HE'S A BIT WEIRD. BUT GOOD WEIRD, YOU KNOW?

SO?

CRAIG, WHAT IF HE'S A CRIMINAL ...?

A CRIMINAL? REALLY?

YOU KNOW, SOME SORT OF EVIL MASTERMIND ... OR A MAD SCIENTIST ...

"THE LODGER UPSTAIRS."
WOW, THAT WAS SOME PARTY. BUT IF I DON'T GET A MOVE-ON, I'LL MISS THE LAST TRAIN HOME.
HELLO. STOP, PLEASE. CAN YOU HEAR ME? I NEED YOUR HELP.
HMM, SOUNDS LIKE A NICE, POLITE FELLOW. GUESS THERE'S NO HARM SEEING WHAT HE WANTS ...
PLEASE. MY LITTLE GIRL'S HURT.
OH, THAT'S A HARD ONE TO REFUSE.
I'M SO SORRY, BUT WILL YOU HELP ME? PLEASE.
HELP YOU?
Of course the poor woman doesn't know that *she's* the one who needs help.

Mumble-Mumble
Craig makes his way quietly to the wall he shares with the Doctor.
HANG ON A SEC, SOPH.
WHAT IS IT, CRAIG? EVERYTHING ALL RIGHT?
ORANGE JUICE GRAVY, DAINTY RHINO, DANCING THEIR HUNGER AWAY.

IN OTHER WORDS, POND, I CAN'T GO UP THERE UNTIL I KNOW WHAT I'M DEALING WITH. IT'S VITAL THAT THIS 'MAN' UPSTAIRS DOESN'T REALISE WHO AND WHAT I AM!
... AND A HEDGEHOG HARNESS, TOO.
IN FACT, I CAN USE MY EARPIECE ONLY BECAUSE IT'S SET TO 'SCRAMBLE'. TO ANYONE ELSE, WE'RE TALKING ABSOLUTE GIBBERISH.
SOPHIE'S 'MAD SCIENTIST' MAY BE CORRECT AFTER ALL. I CAN'T WASTE MY TIME ON THIS NONSENSE.

ALL I'VE GOT TO DO IS PASS AS AN ORDINARY HUMAN BEING. SIMPLE. ANY HELPFUL HINTS?
HMM. HERE'S ONE ... BOW TIE - GET RID!

Time is supposed to move forward … not sideways. It also shouldn't repeat itself. The Doctor, a master of time travel, tries not to become alarmed by what he sees.

INTERESTING. LOCALISED TIME LOOP.
AAAAAAHHHHHH!
TIME DISTORTION. AMY, WHATEVER'S HAPPENING UPSTAIRS IS STILL AFFECTING YOU.

AMY, ARE YOU ALL RIGHT? I THOUGHT I HEARD YOU SCREAM ...
YES, I WAS SCREAMING, THANK YOU. BUT EVERYTHING ...
... SEEMS ALL RIGHT AGAIN NOW.
IT'S ... STOPPED.
THANK GOODNESS!
ALL RIGHT, I'LL NEED TO ACT SOONER THAN I PLANNED ... **AND** LOOK NORMAL.

Chapter 3: The Man Upstairs

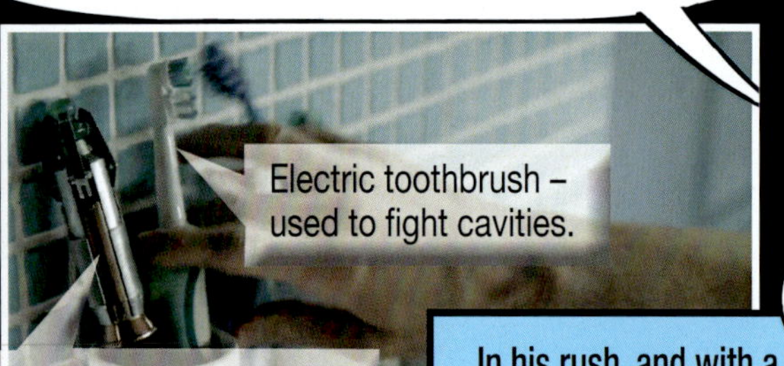

OH, WHAT AM I WORRIED ABOUT? I ALREADY HAVE ONE ...

... WEIRD LODGER TO WORRY ABOUT.
STOP! DON'T HARM CRAIG!

ER, I MEAN, WHAT HAPPENED? WHAT'S GOING ON?
IS THAT MY TOOTHBRUSH?
AH. CORRECT. YOU SPOKE TO THE MAN UPSTAIRS? WHAT DID HE LOOK LIKE?

MORE NORMAL THAN YOU DO AT THE MOMENT, MATE.
I THOUGHT YOU MIGHT BE IN TROUBLE.
THANKS! IF I EVER AM, YOU CAN COME AND SAVE ME WITH MY TOOTHBRUSH!
brrrrrriiiiiiiiiiiiiiiiiiinnng!
EXCUSE ME. WOULD LOVE TO CHAT, BUT THAT'S THE PHONE.

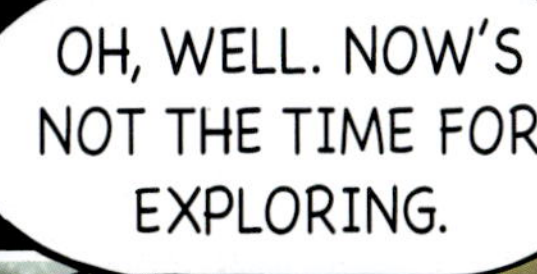

I WONDER WHY THE MAN UPSTAIRS DOESN'T HURT CRAIG ...
OH, WELL. NOW'S NOT THE TIME FOR EXPLORING.

!

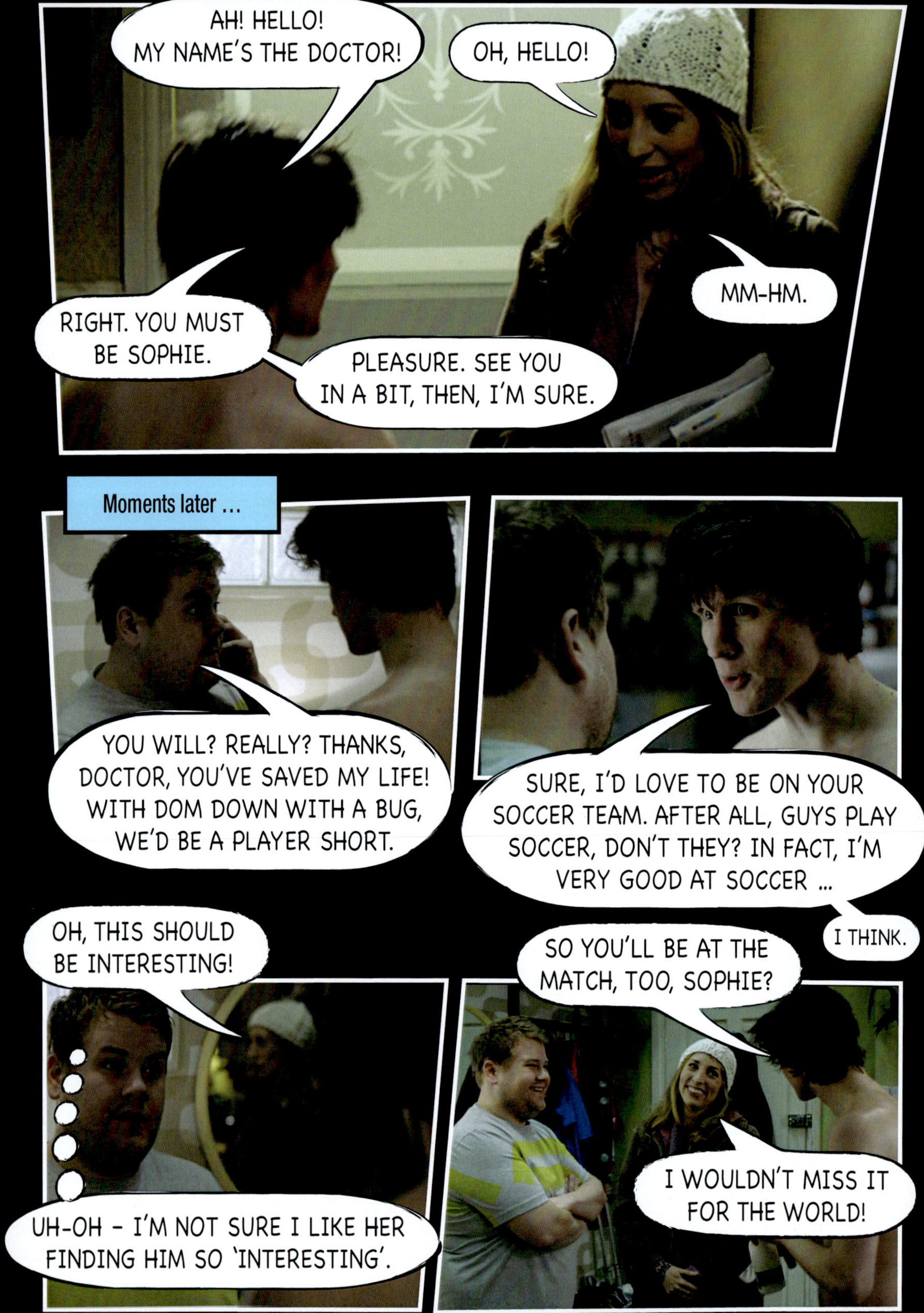

Moments later …

YOU WILL? REALLY? THANKS, DOCTOR, YOU'VE SAVED MY LIFE! WITH DOM DOWN WITH A BUG, WE'D BE A PLAYER SHORT.

SURE, I'D LOVE TO BE ON YOUR SOCCER TEAM. AFTER ALL, GUYS PLAY SOCCER, DON'T THEY? IN FACT, I'M VERY GOOD AT SOCCER …

I THINK.

OH, THIS SHOULD BE INTERESTING!

UH-OH – I'M NOT SURE I LIKE HER FINDING HIM SO 'INTERESTING'.

SO YOU'LL BE AT THE MATCH, TOO, SOPHIE?

I WOULDN'T MISS IT FOR THE WORLD!

The Doctor retreats to his room until a thought hits him.
SOPHIE, WAIT, HOW DID YOU UNLOCK THE FRONT DOOR? THOSE ARE YOUR KEYS OVER THERE. YOU MUST HAVE LEFT THEM LAST TIME YOU CAME HERE.
I - I'VE BEEN HOLDING THEM!
YEAH, BUT I ...

IT'S ALL RIGHT. I DO HAVE ANOTHER SET.
YOU'VE GOT TWO SETS OF KEYS TO SOMEONE ELSE'S HOUSE?
UM, YEAH.
I SEE! YOU MUST LIKE IT HERE, TOO.
The Doctor soon updates Amy on his plans.
KINGS ARMS
SO I'M GOING OUT. IF I HANG ABOUT THE HOUSE ALL THE TIME, THE MAN UPSTAIRS MIGHT GET SUSPICIOUS.

SOCCER? OKAY, WELL DONE. THAT **IS** NORMAL. YOU SHOULD BE ABLE TO BLEND IN WELL.
YEAH. I'LL LOVE IT, I THINK. ALL OUTDOORSY AND SO FORTH.
BUT A QUICK QUESTION ...

SOCCER IS THE ONE WITH THE STICKS, ISN'T IT?

WHAT ARE YOU ACTUALLY CALLED - WHAT'S YOUR PROPER NAME?
JUST CALL ME 'THE DOCTOR'.
THAT'S FINE FOR ME, BUT I CAN'T JUST SAY TO THESE GUYS, "HEY, THIS IS MY NEW FLATMATE. HE'S CALLED THE DOCTOR."
WHY NOT?
BECAUSE IT'S WEIRD.
NO, HE MEANS, WHAT
Soon they are greeted by one of Craig's team mates.
ALL RIGHT, UM, *DOCTOR*. I'M SEAN. WHERE ARE YOU STRONGEST?
ARMS.

The Doctor kicks the ball onto the pitch, and that's how it begins … a soccer match that few who saw it would ever forget …

The Doctor intercepts passes without hesitation.

And he's unstoppable whenever he drives with the ball.

Most importantly, he scores goals.

And then more goals.

Craig, of course, is not thrilled with how his new team mate seems to be outshining him in Sophie's eyes.

But Sophie isn't the only one cheering on the Doctor.

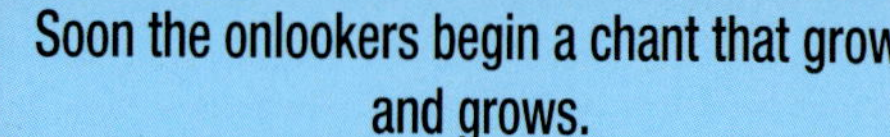

In fact, the longer they play, the more the Doctor simply takes over the match.

Meanwhile, on a familiar street.
SO MUCH TO DO! AND IF I DON'T MAKE IT TO THE PASSPORT OFFICE BEFORE IT CLOSES, I WON'T GET ANOTHER CHANCE UNTIL NEXT WEEK AND –
PLEASE CAN YOU HELP? CAN YOU ...
The woman who is in so much of a rush is surprised to find herself stopping. She wouldn't usually, but it's a **little girl's** voice that she hears.
A little girl who needs help. She sounds so **alone**, so **scared**.
... HELP?
HELLO?
I'VE LOST MY MUM. I DON'T KNOW WHERE SHE IS. PLEASE, CAN YOU HELP ME?
HELP YOU? YOU POOR THING. WHAT'S HAPPENED?
CAN YOU HELP ME FIND HER?
CERTAINLY, DON'T WORRY! I'LL BE GLAD TO COME UP AND ...
... HELP YOU.

With the game over, Craig's team gathers to soak in the victory.

Suddenly the Doctor realises what is happening …

Chapter 4: Monkeys!

Later, that evening ...

THAT'S GOT BIGGER, HASN'T IT?

I DON'T MIND THAT IT'S THERE. I'D STILL PREFER TO STAY IN WITH YOU.

BUT SOPHIE, I WANT TO TELL YOU ...

DOCTOR!

?!

HELLO.

WHAT ARE YOU DOING DOWN THERE? I THOUGHT YOU WERE GOING OUT.

WHOOPS, SORRY. I WAS IN A WORLD OF MY OWN DOWN THERE, RECONNECTING ALL THE ELECTRICS. IT'S A REAL MESS.

HE REALLY IS ON HIS WAY OUT.

UM, I DON'T MIND, IF YOU DON'T MIND.

I DON'T MIND – WHY WOULD I MIND?

DID I JUST MESS THINGS UP? WAS CRAIG GOING TO TELL ME SOMETHING?

And so instead of an evening during which Craig hoped to tell Sophie his true feelings for her, he ends up listening to her confide in the Doctor.

LIFE CAN SEEM SO POINTLESS, DOCTOR. WORK, WEEKEND, WORK, WEEKEND.

SO, THE CALL CENTRE IS NO GOOD THEN? WHAT DO YOU REALLY WANT TO DO?

DON'T LAUGH – I WANT TO WORK WITH ORANGUTANS.

WHAT'S STOPPING YOU?

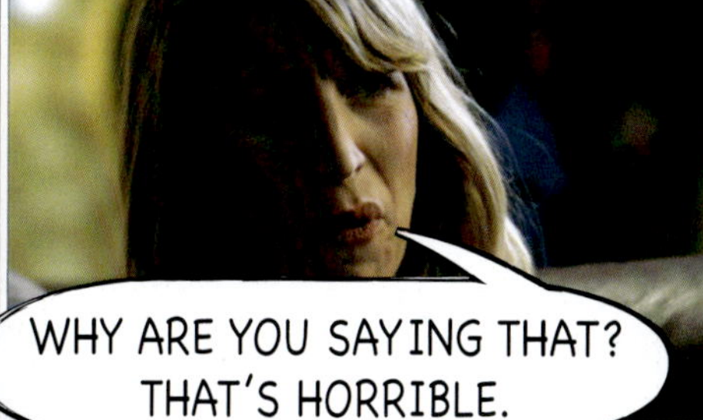

YES, BUT IS IT TRUE?

OF COURSE NOT! I'M NOT STAYING IN A CALL CENTRE ALL MY LIFE! I CAN DO ANYTHING I WANT!

IT'S A BIG OLD WORLD, SOPHIE. WORK OUT WHAT'S REALLY KEEPING YOU HERE, EH?

SO, ARE YOU GOING TO BE TAKING OFF THEN? SEEING THE WORLD? SAVING MONKEYS?

When it's time to say goodnight, Craig tries to keep his tone light. After all, he's only a 'friend'.

WHAT? DO YOU THINK I SHOULD?

YEAH ... LIKE THE DOCTOR SAYS, WHAT'S KEEPING YOU HERE?

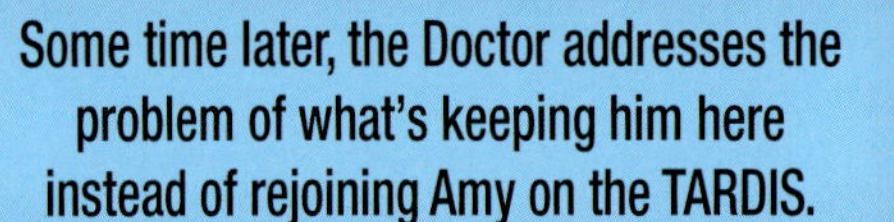
Some time later, the Doctor addresses the problem of what's keeping him here instead of rejoining Amy on the TARDIS.

A master of technology, the Doctor has built a scanner that can help him understand the enemy they face.
SHIELD'S UP. LET'S SCAN!
WHAT ARE YOU GETTING?

If it doesn't bash him in the head, that is.
IT SEEMS THERE ARE NO TRACES OF HIGH TECHNOLOGY UPSTAIRS. IT'S COMPLETELY NORMAL ...
LOOK, YOU SAID I COULD BE LOST FOREVER. JUST GO UPSTAIRS, PLEASE.

BUT WITHOUT KNOWING WHAT I'M UP AGAINST, I COULD GET MYSELF KILLED. THEN YOU'D **REALLY** BE LOST. IF I COULD JUST GET A LOOK IN THERE ...
HOLD ON!

AMY, USE THE DATA BANK, GET ME THE PLANS OF THIS BUILDING - ITS HISTORY, THE LAYOUT, **EVERYTHING**.
WILL DO.
THANKS. MEANWHILE, I'LL RECRUIT ...

"A SPY."
As Craig tidies up, he realises that Sophie was right. The stain *was* getting bigger and bigger.
SO MUCH FOR MR 'I-CAN-FIX-ROT'. I'LL SHOW HIM THAT I CAN HANDLE PROBLEMS IN MY OWN FLAT, THANK YOU VERY MUCH.
SIZZZZZLE
OW!
Craig passes out in his bedroom, and it is in this state that the Doctor finds him when he brings him breakfast the next morning.
CRAIG, I TOLD YOU NOT TO TOUCH THAT STAIN! WAIT, WHAT'S THAT?
NICE GOING, CRAIG! HERE WE HAVE A POSSIBLY POISONOUS SUBSTANCE. "OH, I KNOW WHAT WOULD BE REALLY CLEVER. I'LL STICK MY HAND IN IT!"
COME ON, CRAIG, BREATHE! USE THOSE HEALTHY LUNGS!
GASP!

WAIT - I NEED TO REVERSE THE ENZYME DECAY. EXCITE THE TANNIN MOLECULES.
With that, the Doctor rushes to the kitchen and crams as many teabags as he can into a pot – tannin being a key ingredient in tea …
Soon he is back at Craig's side.
GOOD - HE SEEMS TO BE COMING AROUND.
I'VE … GOT … TO … GO … TO … WORK.
ON NO ACCOUNT. YOU NEED REST.
BUT - BUT - THE PLANNING MEETING. IT'S … VITALLY IMPORTANT.
YOU'RE IMPORTANT, CRAIG. NOW JUST REST AND YOU'LL BE FINE.
07 14
When Craig finally awakens, hours passed in golden silence suddenly give way …
14 45
… to sheer **panic.**
WHAT! NO, NO, NO, **NO!**

PLEASE HOLD, MR LANG.

FEELING BETTER, CRAIG? I HAD SOME TIME TO KILL – NEVER WORKED IN AN OFFICE.

I CAN TELL. WHAT ARE YOU DOING WITH LANG, ONE OF MY BEST CUST– ?

RUN HOME? YES. THAT GIVES ME A CHANCE ...

But soon enough he hears the Doctor in the front hall.

Craig decides to use the peephole to find out who the Doctor is speaking to.

A moment later.

DON'T YOU SEE? I MUST STAY.

NO, YOU MUSTN'T. YOU MUST LEAVE!

I CAN'T GO!

JUST

GET

OUT!

Chapter 5: Showdown!

With an odd lack of anger, the Doctor headbutts Craig.

In a split second, Craig learns everything important about the Doctor – how he is really a Time Lord and all his past adventures. He even learns that the Doctor's appearance has changed many times over the years.

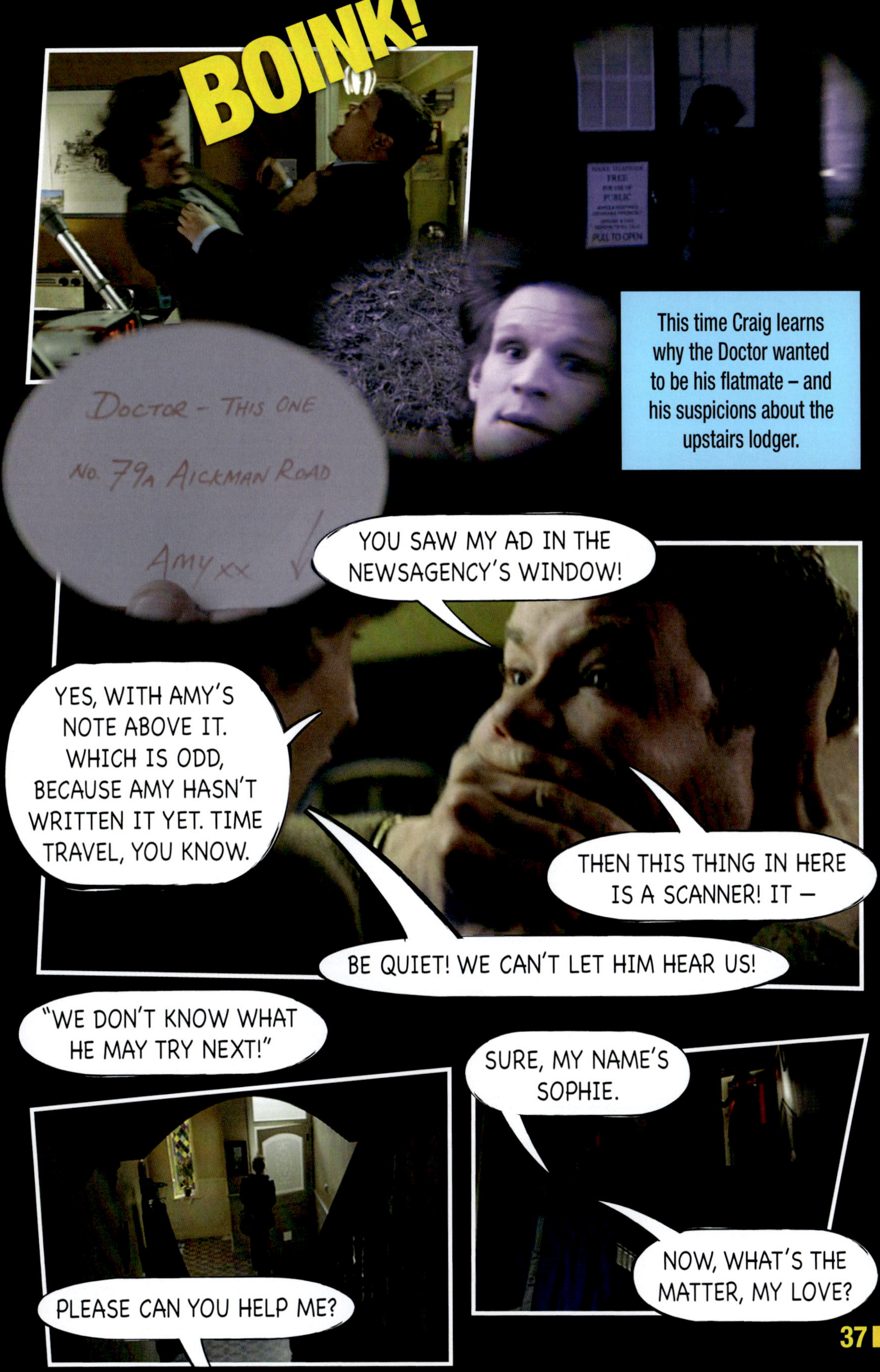

This time Craig learns why the Doctor wanted to be his flatmate – and his suspicions about the upstairs lodger.

PLEASE. WILL YOU HELP ME?
YES, BUT HELP YOU **HOW**?
COME. I'LL SHOW YOU ...
AMY!
THAT'S AMY POND! I CAN UNDERSTAND EVERYTHING NOW!
AMY, HAVE YOU GOT THOSE PLANS YET? I HAVE THE FEELING WE'RE RUNNING OUT OF TIME HERE ...
STILL SEARCHING FOR THEM!
I'VE WORKED IT OUT WITH PSYCHIC HELP FROM A CAT.
A CAT?
AMY, HE'S GOT A TIME ENGINE IN THE FLAT UPSTAIRS. AND HE'S USING INNOCENT PEOPLE TO TRY AND LAUNCH IT.
BUT WHENEVER HE DOES ... THEY GET BURNT UP.
THAT'S WHY THE STAIN – !
CRAAAAASSSHHH!!!
YOU MEAN PEOPLE ARE DYING UP THERE?
AMY, HOLD ON!
The TARDIS again shakes violently ...
smash!
spark!
SIZZZZLE!
I'M **TRYING**!

LET'S GO! SOMEONE'S UP THERE RIGHT NOW!
IT MIGHT BE SOPHIE! SHE SAID SHE'D BE COMING OVER...!
HANG ON, SOPHIE!
DOCTOR!
HANG ON, AMY!
DOCTOR, **STOP!!**
ARE YOU UPSTAIRS RIGHT NOW?
JUST GOING IN!
BUT YOU CAN'T BE UPSTAIRS.
OF COURSE I CAN BE UPSTAIRS!
COME ON, LET'S GO IN!
NO! I'VE GOT THE PLANS, YOU CAN'T BE UPSTAIRS! IT'S A ONE-STOREY BUILDING.
THERE IS NO UPSTAIRS!

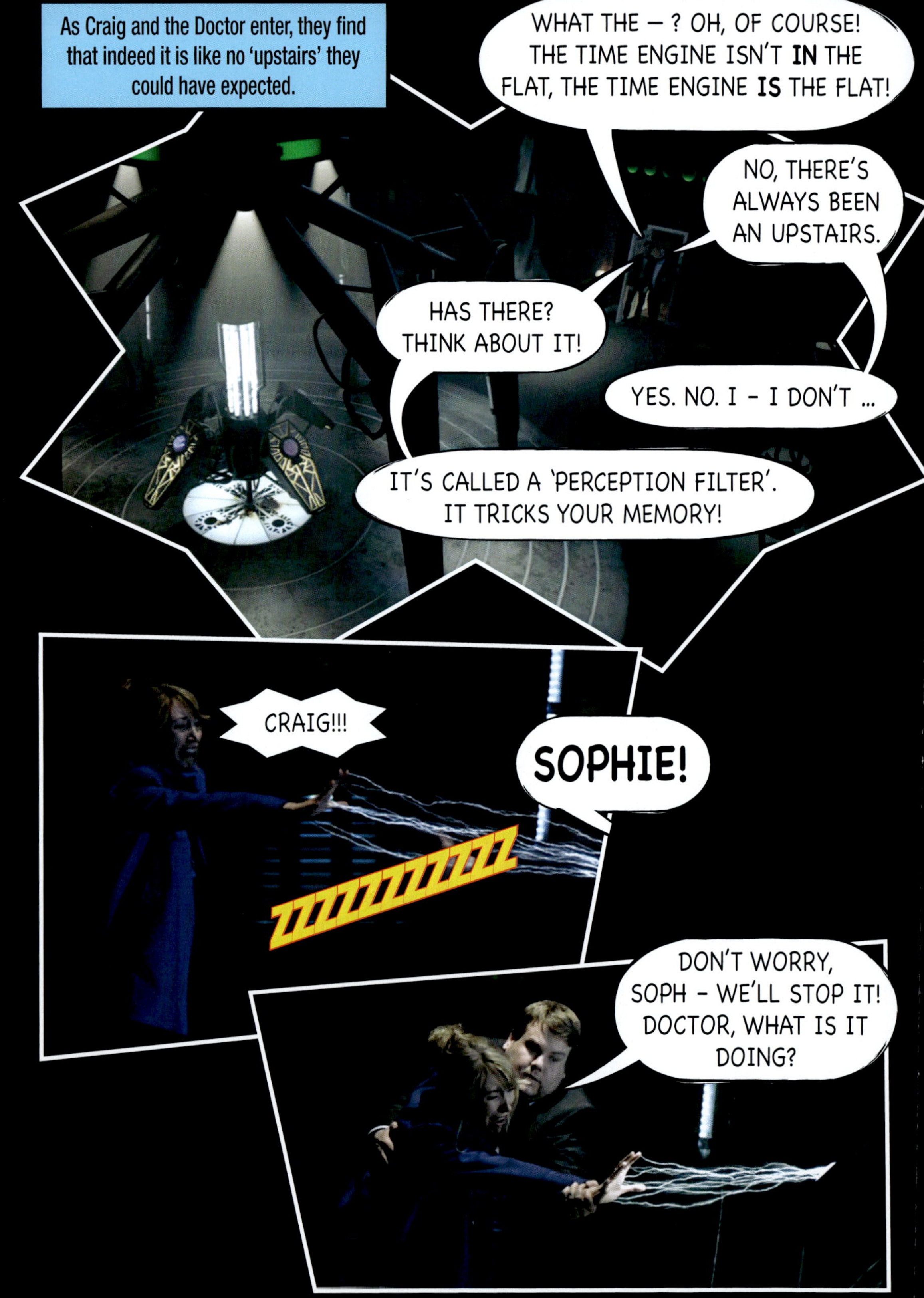
As Craig and the Doctor enter, they find that indeed it is like no 'upstairs' they could have expected.
WHAT THE – ? OH, OF COURSE! THE TIME ENGINE ISN'T **IN** THE FLAT, THE TIME ENGINE **IS** THE FLAT!
NO, THERE'S ALWAYS BEEN AN UPSTAIRS.
HAS THERE? THINK ABOUT IT!
YES. NO. I – I DON'T ...
IT'S CALLED A 'PERCEPTION FILTER'. IT TRICKS YOUR MEMORY!
CRAIG!!!
SOPHIE!
ZZZZZZZZZZZ
DON'T WORRY, SOPH – WE'LL STOP IT! DOCTOR, WHAT IS IT DOING?

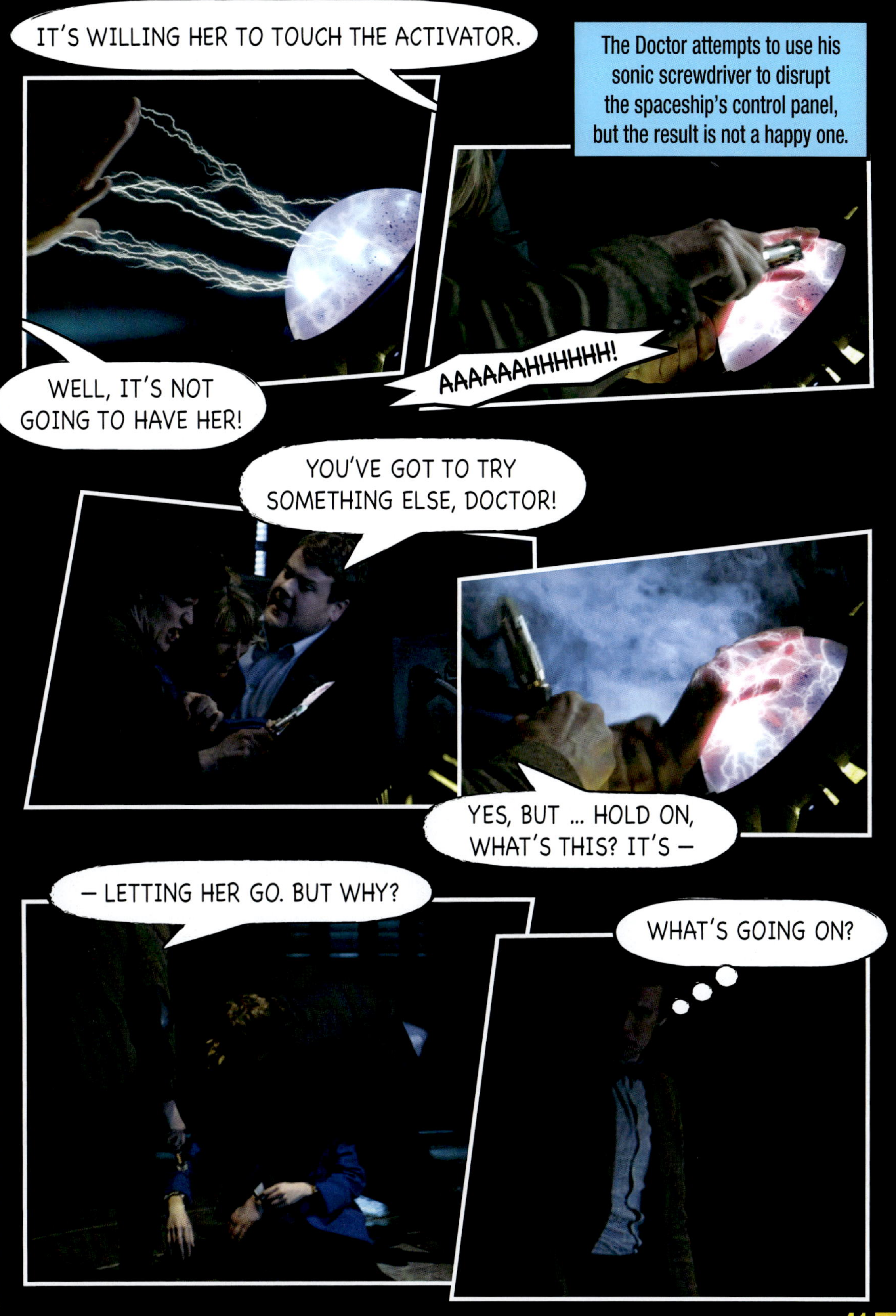
IT'S WILLING HER TO TOUCH THE ACTIVATOR.
The Doctor attempts to use his sonic screwdriver to disrupt the spaceship's control panel, but the result is not a happy one.
WELL, IT'S NOT GOING TO HAVE HER!
AAAAAAHHHHHH!
YOU'VE GOT TO TRY SOMETHING ELSE, DOCTOR!
YES, BUT ... HOLD ON, WHAT'S THIS? IT'S –
– LETTING HER GO. BUT WHY?
WHAT'S GOING ON?

THAT'S RIGHT, SOPHIE. NOW THIS MEANS A CRASHED SHIP, SO LET'S SEE ...

HELLO, SIR. I'M CAPTAIN TROY HANDSOME OF INTERNATIONAL RESCUE. PLEASE STATE THE NATURE OF YOUR EMERGENCY.

THE SHIP HAS CRASHED. THE CREW ARE DEAD. A PILOT IS REQUIRED.

AH, SO YOU'RE THE EMERGENCY CRASH PROGRAM. YOU'VE BEEN LURING PEOPLE UP HERE SO YOU CAN TRY THEM OUT.

HUMAN BRAINS AREN'T STRONG ENOUGH – THEY JUST BURN. BUT YOU'RE QUITE **STUPID**, AREN'T YOU? YOU JUST KEEP TRYING.
17 PEOPLE HAVE BEEN TRIED. 6 000 400 026 REMAIN.

CRAIG, WHAT DOES HE MEAN? WHAT'S GOING ON? WHERE ARE WE?
UM, LONG STORY SHORT – THE TOP FLOOR OF MY BUILDING IS REALLY AN ALIEN SPACESHIP.

THE CORRECT PILOT HAS NOW BEEN FOUND.
YES, I WAS WORRIED YOU'D SAY THAT.

HE MEANS YOU, DOCTOR, DOESN'T HE?

IT'S PULLING ME IN! I'M THE NEW PILOT!
YES, BUT COULD YOU DO IT?
NO, I'M WAY TOO MUCH FOR THIS SHIP. IF MY HAND TOUCHES THAT PANEL, THE PLANET DOESN'T BLOW UP –
THE WHOLE SOLAR SYSTEM DOES!

THE CORRECT PILOT HAS BEEN FOUND.
NO, THAT'S THE **WORST CHOICE EVER**, I PROMISE YOU. NOW STOP THIS!
DOCTOR, IT'S GETTING WORSE HERE!
THE KEY IS THAT IT DOESN'T WANT **EVERYONE**. WHY IS THAT? CRAIG, IT DIDN'T WANT YOU ...
I SPOKE TO HIM AND HE SAID THAT I COULDN'T HELP HIM!
AND IT NEVER WANTED ME BEFORE, BUT NOW IT DOES. SO WHAT CHANGED?
OH, NO! GROAN.
I GAVE SOPHIE THE IDEA OF LEAVING! SINCE THIS MACHINE NEEDS TO LEAVE, IT WANTS PEOPLE WHO WANT TO ESCAPE!
THAT MEANS I CAN SHUT DOWN THE ENGINE BECAUSE I DON'T WANT TO LEAVE. I'M MR COUCH MAN, REMEMBER?
YES! SO JUST PUT YOUR HAND ON THE PANEL AND CONCENTRATE ON **WHY YOU WANT TO STAY!**
CRAIG, BE CAREFUL!
I KNOW, SOPHIE. BUT IF THE DOCTOR THINKS IT WILL WORK ...
... THAT'S GOOD ENOUGH FOR ME!
GERONIMO!
SSSSZZZZZZZZZZZ-
CRAAACKLE!

Now free, the Doctor runs to Craig's side.
CRAIG, WHAT'S KEEPING YOU HERE? THINK ABOUT EVERYTHING THAT MAKES YOU WANT TO STAY!
FOCUS! WHY DON'T YOU WANT TO LEAVE?
IT'S SOPHIE! I DON'T WANT TO LEAVE HER! I **CAN'T** LEAVE HER!
I LOVE SOPHIE!
I LOVE YOU, TOO, CRAIG, YOU IDIOT!
When Sophie slams her hand next to Craig's, signalling her desire to stay as well, it seems that the emotion is too much for the alien craft to handle.
HONESTLY, SOPHIE, DO YOU MEAN THAT?
OF COURSE I MEAN IT! DO YOU MEAN IT?
I'VE **ALWAYS** MEANT IT! NOW, WHAT ABOUT THOSE MONKEYS ...?

OH, NOT NOW, CRAIG! THE PLANET'S ABOUT TO BURN!
KISS THE GIRL!
YES, KISS THE GIRL!!
And so ...

Everything returns ...

... to normal again.
A BIG YES!
Except ...

... for the hologram, that is.
HELP ME.
HELP ME!
HELP ME!

A BIG **NO**! WE DIDN'T TURN IT OFF, SO NOW IT'S DOING AN EMERGENCY SHUTDOWN.
THAT MEANS IT'S IMPLODING. EVERYBODY OUT!

As they rush to escape, the whole house begins to shake.

But soon they are safely watching from across the street …

… as the true shape of the alien space ship finally **appears** …

… and **disappears**.

And so a few minutes later …

HEY, WAIT UP!
ARE YOU TRYING TO SNEAK OFF?
YES, WELL, I FELT THAT YOU TWO WOULD FINALLY WANT SOME TIME ALONE.
TRUE. BUT I ALSO WANT YOU TO KEEP THESE KEYS. THANK YOU.
BECAUSE I MIGHT POP BACK. IS THAT IT?
WHATEVER YOU TWO DO, I WON'T FORGET YOU. THANK YOU FOR EVERYTHING.
YES, BUT IF YOU DO, MAKE IT SOON. OTHERWISE WE MIGHT BE IN PARIS.
OR IN THE JUNGLE WITH THE MONKEYS.
AH, AMY, IT'S SO GOOD TO BE BACK!
AND IT'S GOOD TO HAVE YOU BACK! WHERE TO NOW? ANOTHER EXCITING ADVENTURE IN SOME FAR CORNER OF THE UNIVERSE?
NOT SO FAST! FIRST WE NEED TO GO BACK IN TIME THREE DAYS.
ONLY THREE DAYS? BUT WHY?
BECAUSE YOU STILL NEED TO LEAVE ME THAT NOTE AT THE NEWSAGENCY!